A STORYTELLER BOOK

Easter Stories

BOB HARTMAN

Illustrated by Nadine Wickenden

LION
CHILDREN'S

Published by
Lion Hudson Limited
Wilkinson House, Jordan Hill Business Park,
Banbury Road, Oxford OX2 8DR, England
www.lionhudson.com
ISBN 978 0 7459 7809 3

First edition 2005

A catalogue record for this book is available from the British Library

Printed and bound in the UK, January 2019, LH26

Contents

Introduction

I didn't get it. I just didn't get it. Every Easter it was the same. On Palm Sunday, we'd go to church and celebrate the fact that the crowds had clapped and cheered for Jesus and called him their king. Then only five days later, we'd be sitting in the same place, all solemn-faced, remembering how that same crowd had clamoured for his death.

What happened? What went wrong? Why did they want to kill Jesus? Those were the questions buzzing around in my head when I was a child, and those same questions prompted me to write this book. My hope is that these stories will help those who read or listen to them to find at least some of the answers.

In my many years as a storyteller, I've discovered that, without question, these are some of the most difficult Bible stories to tell, so in these retellings I have done what I can to bring out some of the lighter, happier and even funnier moments in Jesus' final week. Some of the exchanges with the religious leaders, in particular, are full of humour (though they didn't see it that way!) And, at the back of this book, I have suggested some simple participation activities to help your children enjoy them even more.

Having said that, there is no getting around the fact that, at heart, this is the story of a man on his way to an execution. And so I have also introduced some very simple themes and devices to help quieten things down as the stories move towards those serious and solemn moments.

Finally, of course, there is plenty of room in this story for celebration too, and I have included a variety of resurrection appearances so that readers and listeners can experience some sense of the wonder and awe that Jesus' disciples felt at the return of their friend.

Whether you're sharing these stories with a child, or a school or a Sunday school class, or simply reading them for yourself, my hope is that this book will help you to better appreciate both the Easter season and the journey of the one who rode down a hill into Jerusalem, went up another hill to his death, and rose to ascend from yet another hill into the heavens.

Bob Hartman

1

Jesus Rides a Donkey Down the Hill

'I need a donkey,' said Jesus to his friends.
'I need a donkey.' (Hee-Haw!)
'And if the owner of the donkey should ask you
  what you're doing,
Say I need to ride the donkey down the hill.
I need to ride the donkey down the hill.'

So Jesus' friends went to find a donkey.
They went to find a donkey. (Hee-Haw!)
And when the owner asked, they simply answered,
'Jesus needs to ride the donkey down the hill.
Jesus needs to ride the donkey down the hill.'

Then Jesus' friends put a cloak onto the donkey.
A cloak, not a saddle. (Hee-Haw!)
Then Jesus climbed on and headed for Jerusalem.
And Jesus rode the donkey down the hill.
And Jesus rode the donkey down the hill.

The people were surprised when they saw him
    on the donkey,
When they saw him on the donkey. (Hee-Haw!)
Then they remembered a promise – a promise
    from a prophet
About a king who rides a donkey down the hill.
About a king who rides a donkey down the hill.

So the people cheered when they saw him
    on the donkey.
The people cheered. (Hooray!)
They cried, 'Hosanna! Save us, Lord!'
As Jesus rode the donkey down the hill.
As Jesus rode the donkey down the hill.

Then they laid their cloaks in front of the donkey,
And they laid down palm branches too. (Hooray!)
And they treated Jesus just like a king.
As Jesus rode the donkey down the hill.
As Jesus rode the donkey down the hill.

But the religious leaders grumbled and groaned.
They cursed and swore and moaned.
  (Moan! Moan!)
'You're no king!' they cried. 'You're nobody
  special!'
As Jesus rode the donkey down the hill.
As Jesus rode the donkey down the hill.

'Say what you like!' called Jesus to the leaders.
'Be as stubborn as donkeys!' (Hee-Haw!)
'If these stones could speak, they'd join with
  the people
And cheer the one who rides the donkey down
  the hill.
And cheer the one who rides the donkey down
  the hill!'

2

Jesus Knocks Down the Tables in the Temple

When Jesus arrived in Jerusalem, the first thing he did was visit the Temple. But when he got there, he saw something that made him very sad.

There were poor people, who had come a long way to worship God. They had doves with them, the very best they could find, and they wanted to give them to God, as a way of saying thank you for his love.

But the men who worked at the Temple would not let them do that.

'We're very sorry,' they said, 'but the doves you have brought are not good enough for God. You have to buy these "special" Temple doves.'

And they pointed to a bench that was covered with cages.

The poor people set down their own doves and fumbled around for what few coins they could find.

'We're very sorry,' said the temple workers once again. 'We don't take ordinary coins here. You have to use "special" Temple money to buy the "special" Temple doves!' And they pointed to a table that was covered with coins.

So the poor people sighed and changed their money. But for every two coins they gave, they only got one coin back.

'You've cheated us!' they cried.

And the temple workers just grinned. 'We're very sorry,' they said for the third time. 'But those are the rules. Now stop your moaning and get on with your business.'

Jesus was no longer sad. No, Jesus was angry now. In fact, he was furious! These poor people had come simply to worship God, and they were being cheated every way they turned.

So Jesus did something. Something that no one

expected. Something that no one had ever done before.

He turned over the tables of the money-changers. He knocked down the benches full of doves. And as the coins clattered onto the floor and the birds flew free from their cages, Jesus cried, 'God's Temple should be a place of prayer, but you have made it a hideout for cheats and thieves!'

The poor people cheered when they heard what Jesus said.

But the money-changers and the bird-sellers and all the other cheats were very angry.

And so were the religious leaders, who had been watching all along.

'We need to do something about this man,' they grumbled. 'We need to stop him now!'

And that was just the beginning of Jesus' troubles.

3

Grapes and Farmers and Religious Leaders

The religious leaders followed Jesus everywhere he went. They listened to everything he said. And they watched everything he did. They were looking for a reason to arrest him.

So Jesus warned the people about them.

'Watch out for the religious leaders,' he said. 'They want you to think that they are serving God – that they are good and holy men. But they are really just interested in what they can get for themselves – power, money and praise.'

And then Jesus told the people a story:

Once upon a time, there was a man who owned a vineyard. He wanted to go away on a long trip, so he made a deal with some local farmers.

'Take care of my vineyard for me,' he said. 'And you can have most of the grapes. But because it is my vineyard, I want you to save some of the grapes for me as well. At harvest time, I'll send one of my servants to collect them.'

So the man went away. The farmers took care of the vineyard. And when harvest time came, the man sent a servant for his share of the grapes.

'I've come to collect my master's grapes,' the servant said.

But the farmers just laughed.

'Why should we give you the grapes?' they asked. 'Your master is far, far away!'

And they beat the servant up and sent him away with no grapes at all!

So the man who owned the vineyard sent another servant.

'I've come to collect my master's grapes,' the servant said.

And the farmers laughed again.

'You're not getting any grapes either,' they sneered. And they beat that servant up as well and sent him home empty-handed.

So the man sent a third servant. But the same thing happened again!

'I've come to collect my master's grapes,' the servant said.

The farmers laughed louder than ever, and they beat the servant till he ran away.

The man who owned the vineyard had one last idea.

'I will send my son,' he said. 'Surely the farmers will respect him and give him the grapes.'

But when the farmers saw the son walking towards the vineyard, they had a different idea.

'It's his son!' they whispered. 'His only son. If we kill him, there will be no one to inherit the vineyard when the master dies, and we can take it as our own!'

So that's what they did. Having made their evil plan, they lay in wait for the master's son. They grabbed hold of him. They dragged him out of the vineyard. And then they put him to death!

Jesus stopped and looked past the crowd, right to

the back, where the religious leaders were standing.

'So what do you think the master will do with these men?' he asked. 'These men whom he trusted, but who used their position to get what they could for themselves. He will come and throw them out of his vineyard – that's what he'll do – and give their jobs to someone else!'

The religious leaders were furious!

'He's talking about us,' they whispered. 'He thinks that we're like the farmers in the story!'

They wanted to arrest Jesus – they really did! But they could see that the people liked him. So they decided, instead, to wait. To wait and to plan.

Just like the farmers in the story, in fact. Just like the farmers in the story!

4

A Taxing Question

The religious leaders were angry with Jesus. They were jealous of him too.

'If the people listen to him,' they moaned, 'they may not do what we tell them any more. We won't be nearly so important or powerful.'

So they decided to test Jesus – to ask him hard questions in the hope that he would give the wrong answers and that the people would stop listening to him. They felt sure they could catch him out.

'I've got a good question!' said one of the religious leaders. 'The people hate the Romans, because the Romans rule our country and treat us so badly. Let's ask Jesus if he thinks it's right to pay taxes to the Roman leader, Caesar.'

'Brilliant!' said another religious leader. 'The people will not like it if Jesus says that it is all right to pay taxes to Caesar. They believe that God is our king, and that we should honour only him. But if Jesus says that we should not pay our taxes, then we can tell the Romans and get him into big trouble! Either way, we win!'

So, the next day, while Jesus was talking to the crowds, the religious leaders asked him the question: Is it all right to pay taxes to Caesar?

Jesus looked at the religious leaders. He guessed that they were trying to trap him, so he asked a question of his own.

'Can somebody give me a coin?' he said. And when he was handed a little silver one, he held it out and asked another question.

'Whose face is on this coin?'

The religious leaders were puzzled.

'Caesar's face,' they said.

Jesus just smiled.

'All right, then,' he answered. 'Give to Caesar what belongs to Caesar.'

And the crowd booed.

'But…' Jesus went on, 'Give to God what belongs to God as well!'

And the crowd cheered!

The religious leaders, however, walked away annoyed.

'He made everybody happy!' they moaned. 'He's not in trouble with the people or the Romans. Either way, he wins.'

'Well, I've got an even better question!' said another religious leader. 'Why don't we ask him which of God's laws he thinks is most important? Whichever he picks, he'll be saying that the others are not as good. And that's bound to upset someone!'

So they went back to Jesus and asked him their new question.

Again, Jesus looked at the religious leaders. Again, he looked at the crowd. And again, he gave his answer.

'It's simple, really,' he said. 'The first commandment is the most important one – "Love God with your whole heart!" And the second is just as good – "Love your neighbour as you love yourself." Don't you see? All the other commandments – don't steal, don't murder, don't lie – are summed up in these two!'

Again the people cheered. Again, the religious leaders grumbled.

'Any other questions?' asked Jesus.

But the religious leaders just walked away. Jesus had given good answers. He'd passed their tests and they had to admit it. So now they were more angry than ever.

5

Camels, Bugs and Dirty Bowls

'Watch out for the religious leaders,' Jesus warned the people. 'I've said it before, and I'll say it again. Watch out for them – for they teach one thing and do another. It's all just pretend – a show. They act as if they want to please God, but they're really just trying to impress one another.'

'Imagine you had a bowl of soup,' said Jesus.

And the people said, 'Mmm.'

'Now imagine there was a bug in the soup,' said Jesus.

And the people said, 'Urgh!'

'And what if there was something else floating in the soup?' said Jesus.

And the people said, 'What?'

'How about a camel?' said Jesus.

And the people said, 'Whoa!'

'Now you wouldn't want a bug or a camel in your soup, would you?' asked Jesus.

And the people said, 'No!'

'But the religious leaders,' said Jesus, 'would go to all kinds of trouble to strain out that little bug, then quite happily swallow that camel down whole!'

And the people said, 'Yuck!'

'Exactly,' said Jesus. 'They pay lots of attention to all the little, bug-sized details of their religion – what to wear, how to wash, how much of each tiny herb and spice they should give away. But they pay no attention at all to the big, camel-sized things – like loving one another and taking care of the poor. So watch out for them, they'll lead you the wrong way.'

Then, just as if he'd finished the soup himself, Jesus held up a bowl, so the crowd could only see the outside.

'What do you think?' asked Jesus.

And the people said, 'Lovely!'

Then he turned it around so that everyone could see the old food that was caked inside.

'What do you think of it now?' he asked.

And the people said, 'Disgusting!'

'And so are the religious leaders,' said Jesus. 'They look good on the outside – all pious and prim and proper – but on the inside they are dirty with selfishness and jealousy and greed.'

Finally, Jesus pointed across the hill to a cemetery.

'Can you see those bright, shiny tombs?' he asked.

And the people said, 'We can!'

'They look nice, don't they? But what's inside them?' asked Jesus.

And the people answered, 'Dead men's bones.'

'And so it is with the religious leaders,' said Jesus again. 'Shiny on the outside, with all their pretending, but cold and dead inside – dead to the needs of others. And dead to what pleases God as well.

'And the saddest thing of all is that they can't even see it.

'"We want to make God happy!" they say. '"We want to do what's right."' But every time God sends somebody to talk to them – to show them how to stop pretending and let God make them really alive and really good from the inside out – what do they do? They put that person to death.'

Then Jesus looked at the crowd. And his look was very serious.

'Sadly,' he said, 'I think they mean to do that to me.'

6

A Counting Problem

Jesus and his friends went to the Temple. There was a queue of people, waiting to give their offering. They dropped their coins into a hole in the temple wall, and the coins clattered down into a money-box below.

'Come and stand with me by the wall,' said Jesus to his friends. 'I have a counting problem for you. If you listen closely, you can hear how many coins each person has given. Let's see who gives the most!'

The first person was a merchant. He looked very rich indeed. And as he dropped in the coins, Jesus' friends counted them.

One, two, three,

four, five, six,

seven, eight, nine and ten.

'Ten coins!' said one of Jesus' friends. 'Not bad, but I bet someone will do better.'

And someone did. The next man was a lawyer. He was even better dressed. And Jesus' friends had to count more quickly as the coins went clattering down.

Two, four, six,

eight, ten, twelve,

fourteen, sixteen, eighteen and twenty.

'Twenty coins!' said another of Jesus' friends. 'Twice as many as the first man!'

Then a third man walked up to the wall. He was the richest of them all. And what is more, he was one of the religious leaders.

'Watch out for this one,' Jesus whispered to his friends. 'The religious leaders like to send their coins rattling into the money-box just as loudly as they can – so that people will be impressed with what they give.'

And, sure enough, that's exactly what he did. The religious leader reached into his money bag and scooped up a handful of coins. They rattled down so quickly that Jesus' friends could hardly count them.

Five, ten,
fifteen, twenty,
twenty-five, thirty,
thirty-five, forty...

'We give up!' cried Jesus' friends. 'But at least we know the answer to your question. No one is going to give more than that man.' And they turned to walk away.

'Just a minute,' said Jesus. 'There's one more person waiting.'

It was an old woman – a widow, dressed all in black. She pulled two tiny coins out of her purse.

'I wish I could give more,' she whispered to God. 'But this is all I have.' And she dropped the coins – one, two – into the hole.

Jesus looked at his friends.

'Anybody want to change his answer?' he asked.

'No,' said Jesus' friends. 'The third man gave the most.'

'Really?' grinned Jesus. 'But what about the woman?'

'The woman?' his friends chuckled. 'The woman put in only two coins. We can count, you know.'

'I know,' said Jesus. 'But those were the only two coins she had. The others put in more coins, that's true. But they had plenty more in their pockets and in their money-boxes at home. But the woman gave everything she had. Don't you see? It all adds up. The woman dropped in the fewest coins, but in the end she gave the most of all!'

7

The False Friend

Listen. Everything is quiet.

Listen. Even the birds have stopped singing.

Listen. It's late. It's dark. And everyone has gone to bed.

Everyone but the four men in the corner of the temple courtyard.

Listen. Three of the men want something.

Listen. They want it badly.

'We want Jesus stopped,' they whisper. 'We're tired of his teaching, we're tired of his stories, and we're tired of him making us look bad in front of the people. And we think that you can help.'

The fourth man listens. He listens very carefully indeed. He listens to the religious leaders. He listens for the sound of footsteps in the dark, because he shouldn't be here at all. Not here with Jesus' enemies, for his name is Judas. And he is one of Jesus' friends!

'Listen,' he says at last. 'There is something that I want as well. I want money. Lots of it. And if you give it to me, then I will lead you to a quiet place – a place where you can arrest Jesus without fear of the crowds.'

Listen. The men reach into their money-bags.

Listen. The coins clink and clank as they change hands.

Listen. Thirty pieces of silver, and the deal is done.

The religious leaders get what they want.

Judas gets what he wants too.

And in the darkness the devil is laughing.

Listen.

8

Bread, Meat and Stinky Feet

Jesus and his friends went out for a meal.

It was the Passover meal, when they remembered all the wonderful things that God had done for his people – how he had set them free from slavery in Egypt and led them to a land of their own.

They sat on the floor around a low table. They were waiting for the meal to start. Everything smelled sweet – the bread, the lamb, the sauces. Everything but their feet!

They had walked a long way. Their feet were dirty and sweating.

'Phew!' said one of Jesus' friends. 'It stinks in here!'

'Then do something about it!' said another friend.

'But that's a servant's job!' complained a third friend.

And they all started arguing about which of them was the most important.

So Jesus did something that no one expected.

He took off his robe. He wrapped a towel around his waist. And he started to wash his friends' feet.

His friend, Peter, was very upset.

'No, no, no!' he shouted. 'You mustn't wash MY feet. That's a job for a servant. And you are our master, our teacher!'

'That's just the point,' said Jesus. 'I'm your teacher – yes. And if I can wash your feet, then surely you can wash each other's feet. And we can all be servants to one another – with no one more important than the rest.'

So Jesus washed his friends' feet.

Then they all sat down to eat.

And this time, everything – absolutely everything – smelled sweet!

9

A Meal to Remember

Jesus and his friends were eating the special Passover Meal. They prayed and talked and remembered all the amazing things that God had done for his people.

Jesus, however, did not look very happy.

'I have something sad to tell you,' he said at last. 'We all know that the religious leaders do not like me. They would do anything they could to stop me. And now it seems that one of you, sitting here at this table, has agreed to help them arrest me.'

Everyone stopped chewing.

'It's not me. It's not me,' they muttered, one by one. But they all secretly wondered who it could be.

Jesus dipped a piece of bread into some sauce.

'It's the one I give this bread to,' he said. Then he passed it over to Judas.

Judas looked at Jesus. He looked at the others too. And then, without saying a word, he jumped up from his seat and ran out of the room.

Jesus looked at the rest of his friends.

'When I'm gone,' he said, 'I don't want you to forget me.' And he picked up another piece of bread. 'So whenever you come together, this is what I want you to do.' Then he gave thanks to God for the bread, he broke it, and he passed it to his friends.

'This bread is my body,' he said. 'I give it for you.'

Next, Jesus picked up a cup of wine. He gave thanks for it as well and everyone drank from it.

'This wine is my blood,' he said. 'It is poured out for you.'

Then they all sang a song to God and went out for a walk.

Along the way, Jesus looked even more unhappy.

'The religious leaders will come for me tonight,' he said. 'And even though you're my friends, you will all run away.'

'No, no, no!' cried Peter. 'Not me! The rest may run, but you can count on me to stay!'

'Oh, Peter. My dear friend, Peter,' said Jesus, more sadly still. 'It will be worst of all for you. Before this night is over, before the rooster crows to welcome the dawn, you will say that you do not even know me. Not once. Not twice. But three times.'

'No, no, no!' cried Peter again. 'I would never do that!' And all the others said the same.

But Jesus just walked quietly on and led them to a garden in a place called Gethsemane.

10

Sleepy Peter

Peter was sleepy. Very sleepy.

Perhaps it was the special meal he'd just eaten. Perhaps it was the wine he'd drunk. Perhaps it was the walk to the garden of Gethsemane, or perhaps it was just getting late.

'I'm going off to pray,' said Jesus. 'And Peter, I'd like you, James and John to come with me.'

'All right,' Peter yawned, even though he was sleepy. Very sleepy.

They walked a little way in silence, and then Jesus spoke again.

'I'll just be over there,' he said. 'Wait for me. Pray for me. I won't be long.'

'Dear God,' Jesus prayed. 'Dear Father in

Heaven, tomorrow I must die – to take away all the bad things that anyone has ever done. I know it's what you want me to do. But if there is any other way, any way to do this without so much pain and suffering, please show it to me now.'

Jesus prayed long and hard. And Peter tried to pray too. But Peter was sleepy. Very sleepy. And every time he closed his eyes and tried to talk to God, he found himself dropping off to sleep. And so did James and John.

Suddenly, someone was shaking him.

'Peter! Wake up, Peter!' It was Jesus. And he was not very happy.

'All I asked you to do was to watch and pray. Please stay awake. I need your help. I really do.'

Peter wanted to help. He really did. But Peter was sleepy. Very sleepy. And it wasn't long before he nodded off again.

Three times Jesus returned. Three times he found his friends asleep.

But then something unexpected happened. Suddenly, Peter wasn't sleepy at all.

Judas was there! And he wasn't alone. There

were men with him – the religious leaders and
their servants, carrying torches and clubs and
swords.

Judas walked up to Jesus.

'Teacher!' he said. 'Hello!' And he kissed Jesus
on the cheek, just as he'd done every day since

they'd first met. Just as if he was still one of Jesus' friends.

But it was not a friendly kiss. Not at all. It was a signal, so that the others would know which man to arrest.

And that's just what they did. The men with the clubs grabbed hold of Jesus. Now Peter was awake. Wide awake!

He leaped to his feet. He picked up a sword. And he started swinging it about. But all he managed to do was to lop off one man's ear.

'Stop!' cried Jesus. 'Stop right now! This is not the answer. God could save me if he wanted to. But what he wants is for me to go with these men. And that's what I shall do.'

So Jesus went with the men. But what about his friends? His friends ran off in every direction. All but Peter, who followed from a distance. Half awake. Half asleep. Wishing this was all a bad dream. Little knowing the nightmare it would become.

11

A Trial by Night

The men who arrested Jesus took him to the home of the High Priest, the most important religious leader of them all.

'We've got Jesus right where we want him!' the High Priest grinned. 'Now all we need is a good reason to put him to death!'

So the religious leaders held a trial. But it was not a fair trial, with a judge, a jury and people who promised to tell the truth.

No, it was a crooked trial. And the only people asked to speak were the ones who were willing to tell lies about Jesus.

But they could not keep their stories straight – it's what often happens when people lie. And so

Jesus just looked at them all and sighed.

'For three years I have been teaching,' he said. 'Teaching about God. Teaching about his kingdom. Teaching out in the open where everyone could hear what I had to say. I have nothing to hide. Why don't you question some of the people who have actually listened to me?'

One of the religious leaders stepped forward and smacked Jesus in the face.

'That's no way to talk to us!' he shouted. 'The High Priest is in charge. He'll decide what happens here!'

And so, finally, the High Priest turned to Jesus. He spoke very slowly and very carefully.

'We have suspected this all along,' he said. 'But we want to hear it from you. You think that you are the Messiah, don't you? The Special One that God has promised to send us. The very Son of God!'

Jesus looked at the High Priest. And just as slowly and just as carefully, he said, 'Yes. That is exactly who I am. I am the Messiah. I am the Son of God. And one day I will be in heaven, sitting next to God himself!'

The High Priest was furious.

'Did you hear that?' he roared. 'Did you hear what this man said? We need no further witnesses. We have heard it from his lips. This man thinks that he is God's own Son. And according to our law, anyone who thinks that must die!'

The religious leaders cheered. Finally, they had their reason. Finally, they could put an end to Jesus. So they beat him and made fun of him and locked him up for the night.

In the morning, he would die, and all their dreams would finally come true!

12

Panicking Peter

Peter was worried. Very worried.

Jesus had been arrested by the religious leaders, and Peter had no idea what was happening to him.

Peter was loyal. Very loyal.

The rest of Jesus' friends had run away. But Peter had followed him to the High Priest's house, where he watched and waited outside.

Peter was cold. Very cold. So he joined the High Priest's servants, huddled around a fire in the courtyard. And that was his mistake.

'Hey, you!' called a servant girl. And she pointed right at Peter. 'Aren't you one of Jesus' friends? I'm sure I've seen you with him.'

Suddenly, Peter was frightened. Very frightened. And almost without thinking, he shook his head.

'No,' he muttered. 'You've confused me with someone else.'

Then he stood up and walked over to the courtyard gates.

Peter was safe now. Very safe.

Or so he thought. But the servants kept looking in his direction. And after a while, another girl came over to him.

'I think my friend is right, you know! I'm sure I've seen you with Jesus too!'

Peter was panicking now. Really panicking!

'Look!' he said. 'I've told you already. I don't know him. Now why don't you leave me alone!'

'There!' said another servant. 'I thought I heard it. That's a northern accent you've got there, mate. An accent just like Jesus'!'

'No!' shouted Peter – panicking, frightened and confused. 'How many times do I have to tell you? I'm not his friend. I don't know him. I've never had anything to do with him!'

And at that moment – at that very moment –

somewhere off in the distance, a cockerel crowed.
And all Peter could think of were Jesus' words.
'Before this night is over, you will say three times
that you do not know me.'

Now Peter was sad. Very sad. And as the
servants pointed and called after him, he ran
from the courtyard, crying.

And Jesus was, now, truly alone.

13

A Bad Deal

Listen.

The hard smack of a hand slaps across a face.

The High Priest's servants are guarding Jesus to make sure that he does not run away. They have blindfolded him, and one by one they strike him.

Smack!

'Who hit you this time?' they sneer.

Smack!

'Go on. Tell us!'

Smack!

'If you're really God's Son, it should be no problem at all!'

Listen.

In another room, the religious leaders laugh and celebrate.

'Ha, ha, ha! We've won at last!'

'Ha, ha, ha! Jesus is finished!'

'Ha, ha, ha! Soon he will be gone for good!'

Listen.

There are footsteps in the hallway. Suddenly Judas bursts through the door!

'What are you doing here?' cry the religious leaders.

'Who let you in?'

'You've had your money. Now go!'

'Listen!' cries Judas. 'Please listen!

'They tell me you're going to kill him! You never said it would go that far. I never meant for this to happen!'

'Listen!' the religious leaders answer, in return.

'You did your job. You got your money. And what happens now is none of your business.'

'I don't want the money!' cries Judas.

And, listen! He throws the coins onto the floor.

'Take it or leave it,' sighs the High Priest. 'It makes no difference to us. What's done is done. It's too late to change your mind. Now, go.'

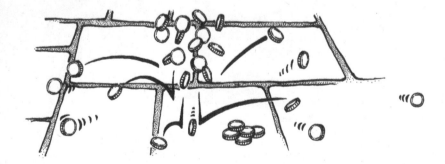

So Judas goes.

Now, listen. His footsteps rattle down the corridor.

Listen. He runs away into the fields.

Listen. He finds a rope and a tree and hangs himself, while the religious leaders laugh and slap each other on the back.

Listen. The devil is laughing louder than anyone.

Listen.

14

No Peace for Pilate

All Pilate wanted was a peaceful life. And he might have had one – had he been a shopkeeper or a butcher or a baker.

But Pilate was the Roman governor of Judea – the country where Jesus lived. And no one in Judea could be put to death without his permission. So on the morning after Jesus' trial, Pilate's palace was anything but peaceful!

At one end of the room, the religious leaders stood and shouted.

'This man is dangerous!'

'He tells the people not to pay their taxes!'

'He says he is a king!'

At the other end of the room, stood Jesus –

tired and sad and alone.

'Is this true?' Pilate asked him.

And Jesus just shrugged.

'I'm a king, yes. In a way, I suppose. But not the kind you're thinking about.'

Pilate looked at Jesus. He looked at the religious leaders too.

'The man seems harmless enough to me,' said Pilate at last. 'I see no reason to put him to death.'

The religious leaders shouted even louder. But Pilate was suddenly aware of another voice. His wife had crept into the room and was whispering in his ear.

'I had a dream about that man!' she said, pointing at Jesus. 'He's done nothing wrong. You must have nothing to do with this!'

Things were even less peaceful for Pilate now. But he had to do something. It was his job, after all.

'I tell you what,' said Pilate. 'Let's ask the people what they think.' And he smiled as he said it, because he had just come up with a clever plan.

Every year, at Passover time, Pilate let the

people choose one prisoner, whom he would then set free.

It was Passover time now!

There was a particularly nasty prisoner named Barabbas who was a thief and a murderer. Pilate would let the people choose between Jesus and this Barabbas. And they would surely set Jesus free.

But when the religious leaders saw what he was up to, they ran out among the crowds and told them to shout for Barabbas.

The people didn't know what was going on, so they did what the religious leaders told them.

'Release Barabbas!' they cried. 'Free Barabbas!' And with all the screaming and shouting, things were now less peaceful than ever.

'But if I release Barabbas,' said Pilate to the religious leaders, 'That means that I will have to…'

'Kill Jesus!' they chanted. 'You will have to kill Jesus! And if you don't, we will tell Caesar himself that you have failed to do your duty. That you have failed to keep the peace.'

Peace. That was all Pilate wanted. And if the death of one man would make that happen, it was a price he was willing to pay. But before he gave the order, Pilate did one last thing. He called for a bowl of water and a towel.

'I wash my hands of this whole business,' he said. And he plunged his hands into the bowl.

The religious leaders shrugged.

The soldiers dragged Jesus away.

Pilate's palace was peaceful at last.

And all it cost was the life of an innocent man.

15

A King, a Crown and a Cross

The High Priest's servants had been cruel to Jesus, but the Roman soldiers were even worse.

When they dragged him out of Pilate's palace, the first thing they did was beat him. They tore off his clothes and whipped his back so hard it bled.

Then they decided to make fun of him.

'You think you're a king?' they sneered. 'Then let's dress you up like one!'

And they put a purple robe on him, the same colour a king would wear.

'A king needs a crown as well!' laughed one of the soldiers.

So they cut a branch from a thorny bush, twisted it into a circle and jammed it onto Jesus' head so hard that blood ran down his face.

'We're still missing something,' grinned another soldier. And he found a big stick and gave it to Jesus to hold.

'A sceptre for Your Majesty!' he sneered.

Then they all bowed down in front of Jesus and chanted, 'Hail to the king. Hail to the king of the Jews!'

After a while, however, they grew tired of making fun of Jesus. And that's when things got worse. Much worse.

They spat on him. And then, one by one, they grabbed hold of that big stick and beat Jesus on the head with it – again and again and again. Finally, they tore off the purple robe, put his own clothes back on him, and dragged him out into the street.

Now it was time for the worst thing of all.

The soldiers laid a beam of wood on Jesus' back and made him carry it up a long hill.

Jesus did the best he could, but his body was

raw with the whipping, his head hurt from the beating, and he was tired, very tired. So when, at last, he stumbled, the soldiers grabbed a man

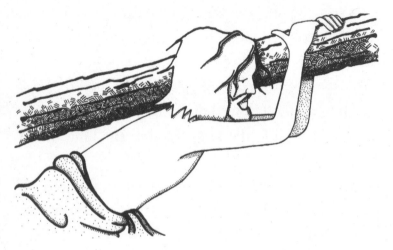

named Simon from the crowd and told him to carry the wood the rest of the way.

When they reached the top of the hill, the soldiers made the wood into a cross and threw Jesus down on top of it. Then – one, two, three – they hammered nails through Jesus' hands and feet into the cross below. They nailed a little sign to the top of the cross, that read: 'Jesus, king of the Jews'. It was meant to be a joke, but the religious leaders did not find it funny.

'No, no, no!' they complained. 'You've got it wrong. He's not *really* the king of the Jews. That's just what he says!'

But the soldiers paid no attention. They lifted the cross, so that everyone could see, and propped it up so it would not fall.

Then they waited for Jesus to die.

The soldiers had done their worst. So what did Jesus do? He did the best, the very best he could.

He shut his eyes and he prayed a prayer. 'Forgive them, Father,' he whispered. 'They don't know what they're doing.'

16

The Crucifixion

Listen!

A thief on a cross croaks at the man hanging next to him, 'If you're really the Messiah – the promised one we've been waiting for – why don't you save yourself, and me too?'

Jesus says nothing. So the thief on his other side answers instead.

'Listen,' he says to the first man. 'Show some respect. You and I deserve to be here. But Jesus has done nothing wrong.'

And, listen. He turns to Jesus, too. And the words he whispers sound just like a prayer.

'Take me with you,' he pleads, 'when you go to your kingdom in heaven.'

'Listen,' Jesus answers the man, 'today you will be with me in Paradise.'

Then listen.

Jesus has something else to say. His heart is breaking, his body aching, but there's just one more thing to be done.

'John!' he calls to his friend. 'John!' And the breath is so hard to find. 'Take care of my mother, will you? Treat her as if she's your mother.'

'And Mother!' he calls. 'Let John be like your son.'

But listen. There are other voices. The voices of the religious leaders. And they are not nearly so kind.

'Jesus!' they laugh. 'Jesus!' they sneer. And the name sounds just like a curse. 'You helped the lame walk and the blind see. So why can't you help yourself?'

Jesus knows why. It's because God wants him on that cross. It's because he really is the Messiah – come to take the punishment for all the bad things that anyone will ever do.

Now listen, because suddenly everyone has gone quiet. It's midday. It's supposed to be the brightest part of the day. But instead, the world has gone dark – dark like night. And it stays that way for three whole hours!

But listen. Jesus has one last thing to say.

'It's finished,' he whispers. 'It's done.'

And that's when he dies.

And that's when the religious leaders get their way.

And that's when his mother cries.

And that's when the devil laughs himself silly.

But listen. The earth rumbles and roars and quakes. And down the hill, the Temple breaks, its curtain torn in two. Now nobody is laughing.

There are two soldiers talking. One of them looks at Jesus, and the words he says sound just like a confession.

'Surely he was right.

Surely he knew what he was talking about.

Surely he was the Son of God!'

Listen.

17

Still No Peace for Pilate

At last everything was peaceful for Pilate.

Jesus was dead. The religious leaders had won the day. The crowds seemed happy enough.

And then someone knocked on his door.

It was a man named Joseph, from a place called Arimathea.

'I have a very simple request,' he said. 'Could I take Jesus' body and give it a proper burial?'

'A proper burial?' asked Pilate. 'But you're one of the religious leaders. Why would you want to do that?'

'Not all of us hated Jesus,' Joseph explained. 'Some of us really did believe that he came from God, but there just weren't enough of us to stop the others. So my friend, Nicodemus, and I want to do what we can to help. Can we have the body, please?'

On the one hand, Pilate was surprised. And on the other, he was really rather pleased.

'Do what you like,' he shrugged. 'It saves me having to deal with it.'

So Joseph and Nicodemus collected the body of Jesus. And according to their custom, they poured spices and perfumes over it and wrapped it up in a linen cloth. Then they placed Jesus' body in a garden tomb and rolled a big stone across the entrance.

Meanwhile, the other religious leaders were calling on Pilate as well.

'What is it now?' he sighed.

'Nasty rumours,' said the religious leaders, 'started by Jesus himself, while he was still alive. From what we have heard, he told his followers that he would rise from the grave, three days after he died.'

'Surely, you don't believe that,' sighed Pilate again.

'Of course not!' cried the religious leaders. 'But his followers do. And we are afraid that they might steal his body and hide it, just to prove that he was right.'

'And so…?' said Pilate, desperate for an end to this conversation.

'And so we want a few of your soldiers,' said the religious leaders, 'for three days – no more – to stand guard over the tomb in case our fears are true.'

'All right,' agreed Pilate, keen to finish the matter once and for all.

'We're very grateful,' said the religious leaders.

'We won't forget this.' And they paraded happily out of the room.

And Pilate? Pilate sighed again – a sigh of relief, this time. For this 'Jesus business' was finally over.

Or at least that's what he thought.

18

A Glad Morning

Listen.

The birds are singing good morning to the sun. It's early. It's the first day of the week.

Listen.

There are footsteps on the path. The path to the garden graveyard.

Listen.

The women are crying as they walk along. Their friend Jesus is dead. Their hearts are broken. They have come to say goodbye.

But listen.

There are soldiers guarding Jesus' tomb. Roman soldiers. And when they hear the women, they leap grunting to their feet, and rattle their short sharp swords.

Now listen.

For next comes a sound that none of them can ignore. It's the sound of the earth shaking. A cracking and a groaning and a roaring sound.

And that's when the angel appears! He is as bright as lightning, with robes as white as snow. And when he rolls the stone away from Jesus' tomb, the soldiers tremble and then faint with fear.

The women are trembling too.

But listen.

The angel has something to say.

'Do not be afraid,' he whispers. And his voice is like snow too – falling soft and gentle. 'I know that you have come to see Jesus. But he is not here. Look, the tomb is empty. For, just as he promised, he has come back from the dead!'

Listen.

The women are crying again. But these are tears of joy, not sorrow.

They turn to leave, and that's when the impossible happens. And their cries of happiness

and surprise drown out every other sound.

For there is Jesus. Standing right in front of them!

And listen.

He greets them.

'Peace be with you,' he says.

And listen.

He asks them to do a very important job.

'Go back to my other friends,' he says. 'Tell them that I am alive. Tell them I want to see them.'

So off they run.

And listen.

The women are laughing.

The angel is laughing too.

And this time, only the devil weeps.

For Jesus is alive again!

Listen.

19

Walking, Talking – and Shocking!

Talking and walking. Walking and talking.

The two men travelled from Jerusalem to Emmaus.

It was a three-hour journey, and because the two men were followers of Jesus, there was plenty to talk about. Like the rumour that some of his friends had seen him alive again!

So, talking and walking, walking and talking, they made their way.

And then a stranger joined them.

'I hear you talking. I see you walking,' said the stranger. 'You sound excited. What's it all about?'

'It's about Jesus!' said one of the two men.

And then, talking and walking, and walking and talking, he explained.

'Jesus was a prophet, sent from God. He did amazing things. Many of us thought he was the Messiah, the special one God promised to send – to save us from our enemies.

'But the religious leaders sentenced him to death. The Romans killed him on a cross. And all our hopes died with him.

'That was three days ago. But this morning, some of the women who knew him went to visit his tomb. And his body wasn't there! Better still, an angel told them that Jesus wasn't dead any more. That he was alive again!'

The stranger listened carefully. And so, talking and walking, walking and talking, he told the two men what he thought.

'You sound surprised,' he said. 'Didn't the prophets say that the Messiah would have to suffer before he claimed his victory over evil? If this Jesus died and rose again, then surely that is exactly what happened to him! I think it shows that he is indeed the special one you've been waiting for.'

Then, talking and walking, walking and talking, they came to Emmaus.

'It's late,' said the two men to the stranger. 'Why don't you stop the night with us?'

And so, talking and walking, and walking and talking, they washed up and then prepared a simple meal.

'Do you mind if I give thanks for the food?' asked the stranger.

'Of course not,' said the two men.

So, taking and breaking the bread, he bowed his head and prayed.

And that's when the two men knew.

The stranger, the man on the road, the one they'd been talking and walking with all afternoon, wasn't a stranger at all.

It was Jesus. Alive again!

But before they could say a thing, Jesus disappeared. He simply wasn't there any more! And they were left alone to wonder.

'We need to tell someone about this!' they cried.

So they hurried back to Jerusalem.

Not talking. Not walking.

But running and jumping for joy!

20

Not a Ghost Story

Two men burst into the room where Jesus' friends were hiding.

'He's alive!' they shouted. 'Jesus is alive again!'

'We've seen him!'

'We've talked to him!'

'We've even eaten a meal with him!'

But before they could answer the chorus of 'How?' and 'When?' and 'Where?', someone else came into the room as well.

But he didn't knock on the door. And he didn't push the door open. In fact, he didn't use the door at all. He was just there. Like a ghost.

And that's exactly what his friends thought when they saw him.

'Jesus!' they cried. But it wasn't a 'How nice to see you' kind of cry. No, it was more like 'Oh dear, we're not sure we like this. We're not sure what's going on here.'

'There's no need to be afraid,' said Jesus calmly. 'I'm not a ghost. Honestly. God brought me back from the dead, and yes, he changed me. But it's still me. And if you come closer and take a look, you'll see for yourselves.'

So he showed them his hands. They even touched the places where the nails had been. (You can't touch the hands of a ghost!)

Then he showed them his feet, and they touched them too. (You can't touch a ghost's feet either!)

And when they still weren't sure, Jesus picked up a piece of fish and ate it. (You don't see ghosts down at the chip shop!)

Finally, when they were calm, Jesus talked with his friends. He told them that he really was the Messiah – the saviour God had promised to send. And he explained to them that dying and coming back from the dead had always been

part of God's plan for him.

'Goodbye,' he said at last. 'I have to go.' (No one dared ask him where!) 'But I'll see you again soon.'

And as quickly as he had come, he was gone.

But not like a ghost. Never like a ghost. Just someone who was alive again – alive again for ever!

21

I Don't Believe It!

'I don't believe it!' said Thomas.

'But he was here!' said Jesus' friends.

'I don't believe it!' said Thomas.

'But we saw him, and we touched him!' they cried.

'I don't believe it!' said Thomas.

'We're sorry you weren't here. We're sorry you missed him. What more can we say?' they asked.

'I don't care what you say,' said Thomas. 'I don't believe it!'

And then he paused.

And then he thought.

And then he spoke: 'I'll tell you what. If Jesus comes back, and lets me see him and touch him –

just like you did – then, maybe, just maybe, I'll change my mind.'

So, one week later, Jesus came back. And this time, Thomas was there.

'I don't believe it!' said Thomas.

'But it's true,' said Jesus. 'Look!'

So Thomas touched the nail prints in Jesus' hands. Thomas touched a wound in Jesus' side. Then Thomas fell to his knees and worshipped him.

'I DO believe it!' said Thomas. 'I've seen him with my own eyes, touched him with my own hands. And it's true! Jesus really is alive again!'

22

Fishing Peter

Peter was fishing. Fishing very hard.

And some of Jesus' other friends were fishing with him too.

Thomas, Nathaniel, James and John, and a couple more.

They were back in a boat.

Back on the Sea of Galilee.

Back to where they'd started – before Jesus had ever come into their lives.

Peter was frustrated. Very frustrated.

It had been a long time since he'd handled a net.

A long time since he'd steered a boat.

A long time – and it showed.

For even though he'd been fishing all morning. There was nothing to show for all his hard work. Nothing at all.

Peter was close to giving up. Very close.

Then someone called from the shore.

'Caught any fish, friends?'

And everyone shouted back, 'No!'

'Throw your net on the right side of the boat!' the voice replied. 'And I think you'll be surprised.'

So they did.

And their net was suddenly so full that they could not haul the fish aboard!

Peter was excited now. Very excited.

For he'd seen this happen before.

'That's Jesus on the shore!' he shouted to his friends. 'Remember when we first met him? He did the very same thing!'

So Peter leaped out of the boat.

Now Peter was wet. Very wet.

He swam to shore, just as fast as he could.

The others rowed behind.

And when they got there, Jesus was sitting in front of a fire – roasting fish and toasting bread.

'Take a seat,' he said. 'You're just in time for breakfast.'

Peter was happy. Very happy.

And then Jesus turned and asked him a question.

'Peter, do you love me?'

Peter smiled.

'Of course!' he answered. 'You know that I love you!'

'Then feed my lambs,' said Jesus.

Peter was puzzled now. Just a little puzzled.

'Feed my lambs?' he wondered. 'What does Jesus mean? I suppose he trusts me. That's it! And he wants me to take care of his friends and followers.'

But then Jesus turned to Peter again.

'Peter,' he asked for a second time. 'Do you really love me?'

Peter was even more puzzled, now. Very puzzled, in fact.

'Yes, Lord,' he answered. 'You know that I love you!'

'Good,' said Jesus. 'Then take care of my sheep.'

Peter picked up another piece of bread.

That's settled, then, he thought.

And then Jesus turned to him a third time.

'Peter,' he asked again. 'Do you love me?'

And now Peter was hurt. Very hurt.

He'd answered once.

He'd answered twice.

Did Jesus not hear him? Did Jesus not believe him?

Why did Jesus have to ask a third time?

And then Peter remembered.

Another fire. Another place. And another set of questions.

'You're Jesus' friend, aren't you?' the servants had asked him.

And three times, Peter had said 'No.'

Peter was ashamed. Very ashamed.

So he looked Jesus right in the eye, with a look that said, I'm sorry. I really am.

And then he gave his answer.

'Lord, you know everything. You know that I love you.'

Jesus looked right back at him, with a look that said, I know you're sorry. And I forgive you.

But all he said was, 'Feed my sheep.'

Peter was happy now. Very happy.

Jesus had forgiven him and given him an important new job.

Peter wouldn't go fishing again for a long while!

23

Up the Hill and Higher Still!

'It's time for me to go,' said Jesus to his friends.
'To go back to my Father up in heaven.'
So he led them from Jerusalem to a place called
   Bethany.
And Jesus and his friends went up a hill.
Jesus and his friends went up a hill.

'Tell everyone about me,' said Jesus to his friends.
'Tell everyone exactly what I've done.
From Judea, to Samaria, to the ends of all the
   earth.'
As Jesus and his friends stood on the hill.
As Jesus and his friends stood on the hill.

'And I'll be right there with you,' said Jesus to
his friends.
'Wherever you are gathered, near or far.
Through the Spirit that I give you, I'll be with
you to the end.'
As Jesus and his friends stood on the hill.
As Jesus and his friends stood on the hill.

Then a cloud surrounded Jesus and took him
  into the air.
Took him high and higher still into the sky.
Some worshipped, some wondered and some
  simply said goodbye.
As Jesus left his friends upon the hill.
As Jesus left his friends upon the hill.

'Why do you stare and wonder?' said an angel
  to the friends.
'Why do you stand and stare into the sky?
In the same way that he left, Jesus will come
  back one day.'
So they praised the Lord and went back down
  the hill.
Off to tell the world, they went back down the hill!

Storytelling Tips

All the stories in this book lend themselves to being read aloud, and many work particularly well with audience participation. Here are some ideas for ways to involve your listeners in most of the stories. Once you have read through the relevant story (match the number below to the story number) you will see how the simple words and actions fit in.

1. Ask the group to say 'hee-haw', shout 'hooray!' and moan at the appropriate places.

2. Ask the audience to say 'We're very sorry' in an officious manner at the appropriate places.

3. Ask your listeners to laugh nastily along with the farmers.

4. You might want to divide the audience into two groups for this. Ask one group to boo and cheer with the crowd and the other to grumble with the religious leaders.

5. Ask the group to echo what you say at the end of each phrase beginning 'And the people said…'

6. Divide your audience into three groups. Ask the first group to count to ten, the second to count to twenty by twos, and the third to count to forty by fives. Lead them in again at the appropriate places.

7. There's no participation here but make the most of the word 'Listen' to ensure the group is quiet.

8. Ask your listeners to go 'MMM!' at the sweet-smelling places, and 'PHEE-UWW!' at the stinky places in the story.

9. Ask the group to mutter 'It's not me' with the disciples and shout 'No, no, no!' with Peter.

10. Ask the audience to yawn and stretch after 'Peter was sleepy' and yawn even more emphatically after 'Very sleepy'.

12. This is similar to the 'Sleepy Peter' story. Ask the group to echo whatever you do at the end of each line beginning 'Peter was…'. Here are some suggestions: 'worried' – face to hands or fingers to mouth and a worried sigh; 'loyal' – a salute; 'cold' – shiver; 'frightened' – fingers in front of eyes and moan; 'safe' – relieved sigh; 'panicking' – a bigger 'worried'; and 'sad' – stick out bottom lip to make a sad face, and sigh.

13. As with story 7 there's no audience participation, but you might want to slap your hands together at the appropriate places, just for emphasis.

14. Divide people into four groups. Ask one group to give a peaceful sigh with Pilate, one to whisper 'He's done nothing wrong' with Pilate's wife, one to shout 'Release Barabbas' with the crowd, and one to shout 'Kill Jesus' with the religious leaders.

17. Divide the audience into three groups. Ask one group to give a resigned sigh with Pilate, one to say 'Not all of us hated Jesus' with Joseph, and one to say 'Nasty rumours' with the religious leaders.

18. You might want to ask the group to stand and shake and stomp with the earthquake.

19. Ask the group to stand for this one. At the 'Talking and walking' phrases ask them to walk on the spot and pretend to have a conversation with the person standing next to them. You can mime the 'taking and breaking' of the bread. Last of all, lead everyone in a 'jump for joy' at the end.

21. Lead the group in a Victor Meldrew-like 'I don't believe it!' every time Thomas says those words.

22. Again this is much like the 'Sleepy Peter' story. Ask the group to echo whatever you do at the end of each line beginning 'Peter was…'. Here are some suggestions: 'fishing' – make a casting motion; 'frustrated' – clench fists and teeth, and grunt; 'giving up' – make a big sigh; 'excited' – wriggle with joy; 'happy' – shout a a big 'woo-hoo!'; 'puzzled' – scratch head; 'more puzzled' – scratch head harder; 'hurt' say 'ow'; and 'happy' shout another 'woo-hoo!'

23. The group will need to stand for this. Lead them in the following actions: 'up the hill' – pretend you are walking up the hill; 'stood on the hill' – hands on hips, look around and stamp feet; 'left his friends upon the hill' – shield eyes and look up; 'back down the hill' – pretend you are walking down the hill.